AUSTIN-HEALEY
100 & 3000

AUSTIN-HEALEY
100 & 3000

David McLavin & Andrew Tipping

Acknowledgements

I would like to thank all those who have been so friendly and helpful while Andy and I have dragged them out of their homes to photograph their cars. As a professional photographer, Andy is immune to the cold but many of us lesser mortals aren't. So thanks to: Julian Aubanel, Roger and Thelma Bakewell, Phil Bawn, Steve Bicknell, John Chatham, Joe and Peter Cox, Philip Dew, Peter Scott Ellis, John and Justin Everard, Don Humphries, Alan Holmes, Peter and Graham Holmes, Alan Neil, John Northwood, Gordon Pearce, Peter Riley, Michael Waterhouse, Ted Warswick and anyone else I have neglected to mention.

David McLavin

Published in 1992 by Osprey Publishing
Reprinted Autumn 1996

ISBN 1 85532 647 7

Editor Shaun Barrington
Page design Jessica Caws
Printed in Hong Kong

Quotations in the text from *Austin Healey: The Story of the Big Healeys*, Geoff Healey (Wilton House Gentry) and *Healey, the Handsome Brute*, Chris Harvey (the Oxford Illustrated Press Limited, Haynes Publishing Group), by kind permission of the authors and publishers.

Right
Restoring Healeys has spawned a whole industry of re-manufactured parts

Half title page
Austin and Healey, a partnership which lasted nearly two decades

Title page
The end of the line – Alan Holmes' 3000 MkIII Phase 2

For a catalogue of all books published by Osprey Automotive please write to:

The Marketing Department, Osprey Publishing, 2nd Floor, Unit 6, Spring Gardens, Tinworth Street, London SE11 5EH

Contents

100

The Big Healey, the archetypal British sports car, was conceived in America. During the early 1950s Donald Healey paid frequent visits to the States to tie up business relating to the Nash-Healey.

He saw that there was a gap in the American market crying out to be filled. As Geoff Healey put it, 'The Jaguar XK120 was giving us a hard time. Bill Lyons had really slipped a crippler on the small car market with his high performance, high value model.' At the other end of the spectrum there was the cheap and cheerful MG T series but there was nothing in between.

The car Donald Healey had in mind occupied this niche perfectly: the first 100 mph car that the average motorist could afford.

As he put it, 'I wanted to produce a very fast everyday road car with genuine sporting characteristics, capable of 100 mph, which would also be exceptionally cheap to buy and easy to maintain.'

The new model's development was spurred on by the worrying rumour that the supply of Riley units, used in the current European Healeys, was about to dry up.

It was also becoming apparent that the Austin Atlantic's lacklustre sales performance meant Leonard Lord, head of Austin, had an embarrassing abundance of A90 engines and transmissions at his disposal.

Donald Healey went to see Lord early in 1951 and told him of his ideas for a new sports car using the Atlantic's engine and gearbox. A deal was struck and, with a supply of engines and running gear assured, work on the project began in earnest.

The concept of the new car was Donald Healey's but it was fleshed out by the combined engineering and styling talents of Barry Bilbie, Gerry Coker and Geoff Healey.

Donald Healey was adamant that good roadholding was 75% frame rigidity and only 25% suspension. He insisted that the frame must be the most rigid possible. The result was a compromise between the traditional sports car, with its separate body and chassis, and the modern monocoque.

It was not wholly successful in achieving the desired aim of maximum rigidity, as any Healey owner will testify. The Austin-Healey's contemporary, the MGA, proved a far better illustration of Donald Healey's maxim.

However, the design still gave the four-cylinder car good roadholding for its time. In modern terms this means that it was fine in a straight line but going round corners was another matter.

The chief design problem, however, was not the handling but building a car light enough to perform well with the heavy mechanical components intended for a much larger car. The A90 Atlantic engine was originally developed as a cut down version of a six-cylinder design for Army lorries. Again though, an acceptable compromise was reached. The prototype 100 had an all-up weight of 21 cwt and a top speed of 110 mph.

Previous page
The Austin Atlantic lacked the flowing lines of the Healey

Left
The A90 engine powered some of Austin's most and least successful cars. The Atlantic's only claim to fame is that it provided the running gear for the Healey

Below
The Atlantic's gearbox was designed for a column mounted gear lever. It took many years before the castings were finally changed to accept a central, floor-mounted gear lever

The Austin-Healey 100 BN1

The Austin Atlantic had been designed for the American market and had a column mounted gear lever. But a sports car with a column shift was unthinkable, so prototype 100s had a floor change adaptor fitted which emerged to the left of the transmission tunnel.

The gearbox betrayed its saloon car origins again when it was found that first gear was too low to use with anything except an over high rear axle ratio, so it was blanked off. However, a three speed gearbox was considered rather a marketing liability so a Laycock overdrive was fitted, acting on second and top.

Similarly, it was planned to fit rack and pinion steering but the only unit available was from the Morris Minor and it simply was not man enough for the job. Barry Bilbie regretted that they never managed to fit a rack and pinion, 'but we had to use existing components to cut costs and we couldn't afford a specially engineered job like Jaguar's.'

Disc brakes were considered for the new car but they were also discarded as too expensive. Production 100s used the 11 in. drums from the Atlantic.

Price was always to be the dominant factor in the Austin-Healey equation, much to the detriment of the car's overall development. Psychologically, the $3,000 barrier was all important to many Americans and the 100 was designed to this limit.

These two factors – the need to keep costs down, and the dependence on the American market – were eventually to kill the Austin-Healey. Justin Everard commented, 'All the time I worked in Experimental, Austin refused everything if it put a shilling onto the cost of the car.' But in 1951 the death of the Austin-Healey was a long way off.

The limited body facilities at the Healey factory in Warwick meant that the bare chassis and running gear were taken to Tickford of Newport Pagnell to be clothed.

Gerry Coker's design received some radical alterations as the body progressed; Donald Healey had the rear wings re-shaped to remove the fins Mr Coker seems to have been so fond of. While the 100's running gear came from many sources, its timeless body was pure Healey and the 'Skipper' showed unerring good taste.

The hood and sidescreens though looked like an afterthought. There is a lurking suspicion among Austin-Healey owners that it must have been five o' clock on a Friday evening when Donald Healey decided the 100 needed a hood.

Once completed, the prototype was driven back to Warwick. After a few deft touches to the front end by a local panel beater, the Healey 100 was ready to make its debut at the 1952 International Motor Show at Earls Court.

The design team were still unhappy with the nose however and the car was discreetly parked behind a pillar. Until, that is, Leonard Lord saw it and declared that he wanted to build it and knock £100 off the price for good measure. Donald Healey agreed and Gerry Coker was sent off to design a new badge for the Austin-Healey 100 BN1.

A batch of 25 pre-production cars was assembled at Warwick while Austin's Longbridge plant tooled up. The early 100s had all-alloy bodies which were rather prone to being dented in transit. Following complaints from overseas customers, steel bonnets and boots were fitted. These were soon followed by steel wings and doors.

The actual changeover point to the mixed steel/alloy body is not recorded but it introduced a major corrosion problem, due to the electrolytic reaction between the two metals. Only the first two or three hundred cars had full alloy bodies.

By July 1953 production had built up to around 120 units per week. All these cars were fitted with Dunlop 48 spoke wire wheels.

Donald Healey is widely credited with reviving the wire wheel but the cost was a long term contract which tied him to the flimsy and troublesome 48-spoke wheel. It was only when Dunlop started manufacturing 60-spoke wheels for MG that they were dropped.

From the very outset the Austin-Healey 100 displayed a number of shortcomings: the hood was never more than shower proof and took two men ten minutes to put up; the gearbox transmitted engine heat directly into the cockpit and the exhaust was noisy and had an unfortunate habit of being ripped off as the rear axle wound up. In the 1950s a straight line top speed of over 100 mph forgave a lot but there were complaints.

A work's competition programme was the Healey's top priority but this did not stop them encouraging private competitors. Racing today is an expensive business with few sponsorship opportinities

A large number of Austin-Healeys are still being campaigned. A 100 Four is seen here in action at the Austin-Healey Isle of White weekend in 1990. Note the bonnet strap. Many production cars were later converted to 100M specification

The first modifications involved changes to the rear springs. The seven leaf springs with a 5 in. camber were soon changed to seven leaves with a 5¾ in. camber to eight leaves with a 3¾ in. camber. Other alterations were made as the result of competition experience.

At the same time as the initial batch of pre-production vehicles was being assembled, four 'Special Test' cars had been laid down. Donald Healey recognised the value of a successful competition programme, for both publicity and development purposes, and was keen to see the new 100 taking part in races and rallies.

The four Special Test cars had larger 1¾ in. SU carburettors, a London taxi gearbox, nitrided steel crankshafts, Birmabright alloy bodies and high pressure overdrive units. Two were entered in the 1953 Mille Miglia, driven by Jonny Lockett and Bert Hadley with Jock Reid and Bertie Mercer respectively as co-driver.

Both vehicles had problems with their throttle linkages on the first stage of the 1000 mile road-race. The spring-loaded ball joints gave way, leaving the throttle jammed in either the fully open or fully closed position.

Left
The leather bonnet strap and louvres shout Le Mans but it is announced more discreetly on the grille

Right
Peter Ellis' beautifully restored 1953 100M BN1. The car is finished in Coronet Cream, a colour specially mixed for the crowning of Elizabeth II.
Peter does not actually like the colour at all but "originality is everything"

Towards the end of the race the Austin-Healey team was also faced with clutch troubles. Just 16 miles from the finish, Lockett's clutch plate disintegrated.

In the post-mortem after the race, the throttle linkage was revised and the clutch plate was redesigned with more rivets securing the friction material to the centre hub.

Almost immediately after the Mille Miglia, work started on preparing three of the Special Test cars for the Le Mans 24-hour endurance race. The hoods and windscreens were replaced with an aeroscreen, the ubiquitous Le Mans bonnet strap was added and a pair of Lucas driving lamps, along with an enlarged fuel tank, were fitted. The pistons were also modified to give extra clearance and remove the split skirt.

The two Austin-Healeys which competed finished in 12th and 14th place, having covered 2153 miles and 2105 miles respectively - a creditable performance for an essentially standard production car still under development.

The lessons learned through racing provided the impetus for a good deal more development work. It was obvious to the Healeys that winning races was good publicity and that the A90 engine was robust enough to stand considerable tuning.

So, the Warwick factory started marketing an extensive conversion kit based on the components used in the successful 1953 Le Mans cars. The full kit contained a pair of 1¾ in. SU carburettors, a revised inlet manifold, a carburettor cold air box, a high lift camshaft, a steel faced cylinder head gasket, a high advance distributor and double valve springs.

Aero screens could also be bought along with a 15 or 25 gallon petrol tank, Alfin brake drums, negative camber rear springs, a larger front anti-roll bar, a competition overdrive, a revised back axle and uprated front dampers. In addition, there was the obligatory bonnet strap and louvred bonnet. The net result was the 100M.

An ambitious racing programme was also scheduled for 1954. It was planned to enter cars in the Mille Miglia, Le Mans and Sebring. The Healeys set their sights high on the engineering side as well.

The still-born fixed-head coupé was conceived with two prototypes being built. And the merger between Morris Motors and Austin, to form the British Motor Corporation, resulted in a new range of rationalised components which it was intended to introduce on an improved version of the production car.

The Le Mans 24 hour race spawned the 100M and it was only fitting that there should be a matching car for Sebring – the American equivalent. Harry Weslake, the great gas flow expert was called in to design a new cylinder head for the venerable A90 unit. He came up with a four-port, alloy head which increased power to 132 bhp at 4,700 rpm (the standard engine produced 90 bhp at 4,000 rpm). The unit also featured a nitride hardened crankshaft, tri-metal bearings and strengthened connecting rods. Further changes included solid-skirt pistons, a high-lift camshaft and a new dual exhaust system.

The 100S, as the car was known, also had an oil cooler to improve reliability and uprated brakes and suspension to cope with the extra power. For the 100S this

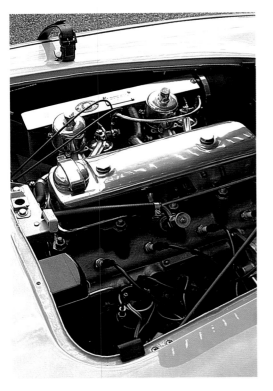

The Le Mans conversion brought the A90 engine's power output up to 110 bhp. Note the carburettor cold air box

The 100 Four featured an ingenious mechanism for lowering the windscreen to improve the car's aerodynamics

Wind-up windows did not appear on the Big Healeys until 1962. This lack of sophistication gave the 100 Four a good power to weight ratio and a top speed close to that of the more powerful but much heavier 3000

AUSTIN-HEALEY HUNDRED
(MODEL B.N.1.)

SPECIAL EQUIPMENT AND
TUNING INSTRUCTIONS

meant the same four-wheel discs as used by the all conquering Jaguars of the day.

Externally an oval grille, a one-piece Perspex windscreen and a huge outside petrol filler cap were all that distinguished the 100S and the 100M.

Weaknesses in the valve train robbed the prototype 100S of victory at Sebring in 1954 but the car still managed to take 3rd place and won the 3-litre class outright - running on three cylinders!

Three 100Ss contested the Mille Miglia but two had to retire. The third car finishing a lowly 23rd much to Donald Healey's disappointment.

The result prompted the withdrawal of the team from Le Mans and a declaration that they would not take part in motor sport again. The feeling was that, unlike the Austin-Healeys, the majority of racing cars were so far removed from their parent production vehicles, that competing against them was not a fair test of the 100's abilities.

But the next year saw the 100S back at Sebring in force. No less than seven were entered with Stirling Moss and Lance Macklin taking the only works 100S to 6th place overall and 1st in the 3-litre class. Four of the private entries and two 100s finished in the top forty.

Much against the Healeys' wishes, Le Mans was reinstated on the competition programme for 1955. A single, specially prepared 100S was entered in the ill-fated race, driven by Lance Macklin with Les Leston as co-driver.

The car was involved in the terrible accident outside the pits when Pierre Levegh's Mercedes crashed into the public enclosure killing him and 82 spectators. No blame was attached to Macklin, who was driving at the time, but the Austin-Healeys were not to return to Le Mans for many years.

Bad luck continued to dog the competition programme when both of the 145bhp 1956 Sebring cars shook their exhaust systems to pieces and had to withdraw. The race was not a complete dead loss for the Healeys though, as a privately entered 100S went on to finish in 11th place.

The race-inspired, limited production 100M and S were the only major evolutions until June 1955 when it was recognised that the standard 100's gearbox was just not tough enough. Austin was quickly persuaded to part with large numbers of its new four-speed gearboxes and the BN2 quietly superseded the BN1. But its production run was to be surprisingly shortlived - less than 15 months.

The four-cylinder 2660 cc engine used in the 100 was being phased out in favour of the new 2639 cc C-Series, six-cylinder unit.

Obviously to keep production costs to a minimum manufacturing volumes had to be kept as high as possible and the Austin-Healey was deemed a likely candidate for the new engine. The BN3 heralded the end of the four-cylinder 100, after some 15,826 examples had been made.

Donald Healey was keen to widen the market appeal of the 100 by providing rear seats. And, as the six-cylinder engine demanded extensive changes to the chassis, it seemed an opportune moment to finally improve the car's ground clearance.

The one and only BN3 produced was built from various components from the Austin parts bin. It had a stretched BN2 body mounted on what Geoff Healey refers to as an L-type chassis.

The Healeys knew how racing success could influence sales and were keen to encourage private competition entries

The Le Mans Engine Modification Kit enables the horse power output of the engine to be increased from 90 B.H.P. at 4,000 R.P.M. to 110 B.H.P. at 4,500.

The effect on performance is marked, and results in improved acceleration and speed. The low speed performance of the engine is not impaired.

Maximum performance will only be achieved by correct and careful fitting of the Kit, and the following installation instructions should be closely followed.

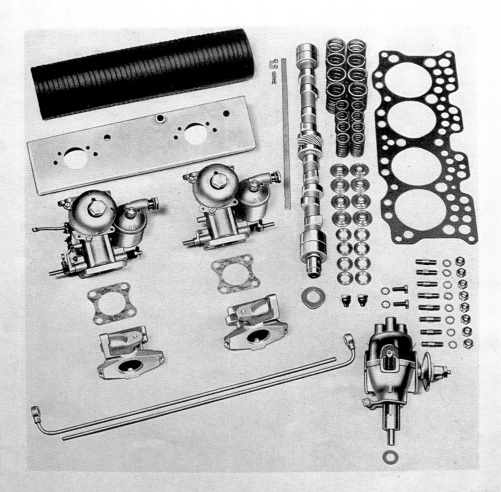

Fitting Instructions

Drain off cooling water and remove the bonnet, radiator, radiator hoses, cylinder head, carburetters, and manifolds. Drain off engine oil and withdraw oil reservoir, oil pump, and distributor. Remove engine mounting bolts (4 at each mounting), detach tappet cover, and withdraw the tappets.

The chassis rails were raised up over the rear axle which was located on quarter elliptic springs with two torsion bars.

The BN3 was noticeably higher at the back than any of its stablemates. The front chassis rails were also raised and a subframe assembly carried the engine which was mated to a four-speed gearbox with synchromesh on the top three ratios.

Why the BN3 never entered volume production is open to speculation but it seems likely that, once again, cost was the over-riding factor.

In the event, the new Austin-Healey 100 Six BN4, introduced in September 1956, was far more an evolution of the BN2 than its radical predecessor. Even so, the Six still incorporated many mechanical and detail changes.

Following the pattern set by the 100S, the Nash-Healey inspired, diamond grille was abandoned in favour of an oval grille. The swage line along the side was extended down the front wheel arch and the bonnet line was lowered. The longer engine meant that the radiator had to be sited further forward, so a bonnet scoop was fitted to clear it. This had the added benefit of improving the air flow and removing the need for the cold air box used on the 100M.

The new engine encroached on the cockpit so the rear chassis outriggers were moved back by 2 ins. to compensate. The body was also extended by some 2 ins. to make room for a pair of BN3 style occasional rear seats, demanded by the American market.

The displaced spare wheel was relegated to the boot with an external fuel filler cap being fitted.

The net result was not, in many ways, an improvement. The relatively good weight distribution of the 100 Four was upset by the heavier engine which was also mounted further forward. The steering box ratio had to be reduced from 14:1 to 15:1 to compensate for the extra weight over the front wheels.

The stiffer rear springs, required to stop the car bottoming when carrying four people, and the chassis modifications also adversely affected the handling. And the 12 bhp advantage of the new six-cylinder engine was largely absorbed by the increase in the car's overall weight. Top speed was up slightly but nearly all the acceleration figures were down.

The Healeys, however, like small manufacturers the world over, were at the mercy of their suppliers so the C-Series engine had to be accommodated.

Even so the uninspiring performance of the Morris-designed unit led to some harsh words at the British Motor Corporation between the Austin and Morris arms of the company.

On the credit side the engine was far smoother and more flexible than the A90 Atlantic unit making the 100 Six easier and more restful to drive. Changes to the styling and fittings also kept the car current. The new sidescreens, in particular, were a vast improvement over the previous items. Weather protection, in general, received a great deal of thought. The revised hood made the car more waterproof and aided its aerodynamics. A more elaborate ventilation system was also installed - at modest extra cost - but it still failed to keep the cockpit cool and condensation free, especially in the wet. Of course,

Left

The 100M engine conversion kit

Overleaf

In its heyday; OAC 783 "taking the Jag on the inside" at Goodwood during the summer of 1954

Austin's production lines could not keep pace with the demand for standard Healeys so many exciting new developments were not pursued. The fixed-head coupé was one of them. At the time of writing, OAC 1 was undergoing restoration, the coupé roof having only recently been re-united with its correct bodyshell

this was less of a problem in the sunshine States, the destination for over 60% of six-cylinder Austin-Healey production.

With the new model just entering production competition experience was again to be the catalyst for further development work.

The British Motor Corporation's great rivals, Triumph were starting to clean up on the international rally circuit. In 1957 it was decided to throw down the gauntlet and a 100S was entered in the 3000 mile Liege-Sofia-Liege rally.

It crashed embarrassingly soon after the start.

Undeterred a 100 Six, UOC 741, was prepared for the Sestriere rally. The virtually standard car, driven by the Daily Herald's motoring correspondent Tommy Wisdom, finished 83rd overall and 10th in its class. Not a spectacular result but a lot of valuable experience was gained into what made a rally car competitive. And what needed to be done to beat the Triumphs.

The Mille Miglia was Tommy Wisdom's next outing in UOC 741 with the car sporting a prototype six-port cylinder head. He finished 37th out of 365 entries and 1st in the 3-litre class.

After this success the Monte Carlo rally seemed the next logical step. Heavy duty front springs and additional leaves at the rear, took up some of the strain caused by the growing weight of rally equipment. They also made UOC 741 faster over unmade roads.

This modification was to lead to the development of the famed 14-leaf rear spring that was to play such a large part in the Big Healey's later rally successes.

Bad weather closed the route from Paris and effectively put the car out of the running. But a precedent had been set and rallying was to feature more and more on the competition programme.

Three cars were also entered at Sebring in 1957. These vehicles again featured the revised cylinder head with six ports and a separate, alloy inlet manifold. On the standard Six, the inlet manifold was cast as a gallery in the cylinder head. Triple, dual choke Webers and nitride hardened crankshafts completed the race preparations and raised power output to 150 bhp.

Two of the cars suffered broken connecting rods while the third was damaged after hitting the kerb on a bend. Amazingly it still finished in 26th position.

The race had revealed a design fault with the connecting rod, highlighting the value of competition participation.

Similarly, the 1958 event uncovered problems with the gearbox, input shaft, oil seal. A combination of high revolutions and fierce braking - standard racing conditions - forced lubricant past the scroll type oil seal, contaminating the clutch. The solution was to fit moulded rubber, lipped seals, a modification carried over into production vehicles.

Despite this problem, the three cars in the Austin-Healey team still finished 14th, 17th and 22nd and took the manufacturer's prize.

On the mountains too, the Big Healeys were beginning to assert themselves. Flushed with Tommy Wisdom's success the previous year, the British Motor Corporation had decided to go for complete domination of the rally scene.

The result was an Alpine Cup for Bill Shepherd and John Williamson and a Coupe des Dames award for Pat Moss, Stirling's sister, and Ann Wisdom in the 1958 Alpine rally. Pat and Anne went on to decisively beat the dominant Mercedes 300SLs to take a Coupes des Dames, manufacturers and team awards in the Liege rally.

Two coupé prototypes were built. One was eventually fitted with a four cylinder engine uprated to S specification while the other was powered by an early six cyclinder unit

The 100S. Only 55 examples were made

When the new, six port cylinder head was fitted to standard production cars with twin 1 ¾ in. SUs, a modified distributor and an increased compression ratio the result was a modest rise in power output to 117 bhp. The new cylinder head brought with it a change of designation and the 100 Six BN6 was now restored to the performance levels of the BN2 model. But there were demands for still more power, especially from America. As the vast majority of Austin-Healeys produced were export models destined for the States these demands were quickly answered.

Left

Harry Weslake virtually redesigned the 100's engine. On the 100S the exhaust and inlet ports are on the right-hand-side of the engine, not the left as is usually the case

Below

The 100S was a thorough bred racer. Note the high capacity fuel filler and racing seats

Above
The 100S featured a heavy duty oil-cooler

Right
On later competition cars a more refined model was fitted

Preparing work's cars to rally specification often involved the judicious use of of a blunt instrument. A little more care was taken with this hand-made inlet manifold

Above
The long range fuel tank needed for endurance racing

Left
The 100S had disc brakes all round. Unfortunately the whole caliper had to be dismantled to change the pads which entailed bleeding the brakes

Right

The one and only BN3 was the first Austin-Healey fitted with the 2639 cc C-Series engine. The integral inlet manifold used on the C-Series is clearly visible here. It made balancing the carburettors a difficult business

Overleaf

By cross referencing the engine and chassis numbers, the Driver Vehicle Licensing Centre in Swansea has identified this car as the BN3 six-cylinder prototype. It has also been re-allocated its original registration number, NWD 977

The BN3 featured a radically different rear suspension set up which would have improved ground clearance enormously

The C-Series engine was longer than the A90 unit it replaced. The problem was solved in the BN3 by mounting the engine on a separate subframe assembly

Right
The 100 Six BN4 introduced a number of stylng changes, many necessitated by the new engine. In manufacturing terms, it was obviously easier to put a scoop in the bonnet than change the front suspension

Overleaf
Lengthening the body to accommodate the rear seats did not damage the 100's good looks

Anyone who has had to travel in the back of a 100 Six knows the seats were only designed for legless adults and small children. Note the small child in the back

Roger Bakewell's 100 Six is unusual in having a fully trimmed boot

Above
This 'more elaborate' ventilation system bacame a common feature of the works rally cars. Later vehicles used the roof vent from the Mini van

Left
The integral stop, rear and indicator light used on most of the Big Healey's can cause modern drivers some problems

Right
In 1958 a publicity car was also converted to current rally specification for an attempt at the seven day distance record by the Cambridge University Automobile Club. They were successful and VOK 490 is one of the few record breaking cars still in existence

Above

The rally cars were stripped of all excess weight to improve performance. The result was a highly functional interior

Right

Modifications tended to be carried out on an ad hoc basis, usually with a large hammer. Here the number plate has been cut away to improve the airflow to the oil cooler

A 100 Six is seen on Tower Bridge art the start of the 1990 Pirelli Marathon

Left
Using the door as an air-brake was a technique often employed under racing conditions. Racing tended to expose flaws. In this case body flex which released the door latch

Below
SMO 745 was driven by many of the top rally drivers of the era including Pat Moss, Peter Riley and the Morley brothers

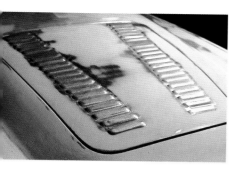

Left
High underbonnet temperatures were a constant problem. Louvring the bonnet was one solution

Below
Some of the famous names in the Healey's chequered career

3000

The easiest way to improve output is to increase cubic capacity. The tough and reliable C-Series engine was a good candidate for boring-out. Enlarging the capacity to 2912 cc, significantly the engine size used by the 1958 Sebring cars, brought the power output up to 124 bhp and made the Healey far more competitive in the up-to-3-litre class. The larger bore also improved engine breathing, making it less sensitive to ignition settings and mixture adjustment.

In the summer of 1959 the first Austin-Healey 3000s appeared. Two-seat models were referred to as BN7s while the four-seater was known as the BT7.

Externally the new models differed little from the BN6 but some significant changes were made to cope with the extra power. Twin-piston, Girling disc brakes replaced the front drums and a larger clutch was fitted.

These engine and brake developments made the 3000 the most advanced car in the Austin range and they were soon applied to other models.

The year had its ups and downs on the competition front. The single car entered in the RAC Rally crashed and the complete team in the Alpine were beaten by Triumph TR3s. But Peter Riley and Rupert Jones evened the score a little by taking a 3000 to its first international victory in the Liege rally while Pat Moss and Ann Wisdom finished second in the German.

Rally success continued the next year with with Pat and Ann taking the honours in the Liege-Rome-Leige. They also took the Coupes des Dames in the Geneva and Tulip rallies as well as finishing second in the Alpine. The year closed with ten out of a possible 14 international class wins, a fantastic publicity coup for the Big Healeys.

Sebring seems to have been the Healeys' favourite venue but 1960 was not a good year for the road racers. Two of the three cars entered were plagued by gearbox problems which left only top gear working.

Competition experience, again pointed the way forward in May 1961 when the triple carburettor layout, used on works cars the year before, was applied to production vehicles. The resulting 3000 MkII carried three 1½ in. SU carburettors mounted on a revised inlet manifold. The valve springs were also modified along with the camshaft. Peak power was now 131 bhp at 4,750 rpm. Servo-assisted brakes were also offered as an option for the first time.

There were few styling changes to differentiate the MkI and the MkII. The radiator grille was altered with vertical bars replacing the horizontal slats of the earlier 3000s. In the American consumer led market, detail changes which announced the car was this year's model were all important. There was also the perception that horizontal slats were vulgar.

As Geoff Healey put it, 'The American public were conditioned to frequent model changes. American manufacturers usually introduced a new model every year or else included some easily identifiable changes. It was felt that change was necessary to encourage owners to buy a new car.

'The USA was by far the biggest market. Under these circumstances, it's hardly surprising that we gave most consideration to what the USA required.'

Sales of the new model benefitted from another good year of competition successes with Austin-Healeys scoring class wins in the Monte Carlo, RAC and Liege rallies. The Liege win was especially good for publicity as it was gained over one of the toughest courses ever. Only eight cars finished out of 85. The fact that three of the retirements were the other works Austin-Healeys somehow was not mentioned in the sales literature.

The Morley brothers also took the Alpine rally despite losing second gear during the mountainous Cap Shelmont special stage. On the racing circuit the famed DD 300 was running well at Le Mans until it had to retire with engine trouble. Under the new ownership of Bob Olthoff the car ran a close second to

Previous page
More and more left-hand-drive Healeys are being imported back into this country as demand for the marque increases

Below
Wind in the hair motoring has always been one of the appeals of the Big Healey. John Northwood is seen here driving his proverbial 'found in a barn derelict'

the winning Ferrari 250 GTO in the South African Rand nine hour race.

Production Austin-Healeys continued to benefit from carried-over racing technology but the tripple carburettor set up was soon dropped from the 3000 specification. In ideal conditions they improved power output and cut fuel consumption. But balancing three carburettors was beyond most mechanics of the time and in April 1962 the 3000 reverted to twin carburettors.

Other alterations were also introduced at the same time. A new gearbox casing finally answered criticisms that excessive pressure was needed to change gear. Gear selection had always been a problem because of the awkward floor adaptor and long, dog-legged lever.

Rally experience brought with it other modifications. The transmission tunnel was changed to fibre glass, bringing the first significant advance in cockpit cooling. Stiffer front springs and modified damper settings improved road holding.

Production of this latest incarnation of the Austin-Healey, the 3000 MkIIA BJ7 centred on the four-seater, the two-seater being discontinued. The rear seats were given more legroom and a wrap-around windscreen was fitted.
The improved aerodynamics made the new model even faster than the previous triple carburettor version. It was also endowed with more in the way of creature comforts and wind-up windows with quarter lights were fitted as standard.

The development process did not work in reverse and wind-up windows, which added weight, did not feature on the thorough-bred race and rally cars. But even without the benefit of this major technical advance, the Big Healeys were still highly competitive.

In 1962, the 3000 made one of its rare appearances at the Monte Carlo rally, finishing eighteenth overall. The Tulip's 'class improvement' marking system again worked against the Austin-Healeys. Despite the Morley brothers putting in the fastest aggregate time in the eliminating tests, the team had to be content with first and second in class.

The Alpine rally that year belonged to the Healeys. The Morleys won the event outright for the second time running. Pat Moss and her new co-driver Pauline Mayman were placed third with Dave Seigle-Morris and Tony Ambrose finishing eighth.

The Liege again tested the Austin-Healeys to the limits. A broken rear spring mounting cost Dave Siegle-Morris' an hour and a half but running repairs put him back in the race and allow him to achieve a personal ambition and finish three Lieges in a row.

The following year was a disappointing one for the Abingdon team. The Morley twins were keen to complete a third consecutive penalty-free Alpine to win one of the very rare Coupes d'Or. Unfortunately, while in the lead on the final night, an experimental axle assembly failed putting the Morleys out of the running.

The 1963 Alpine was particularly bad for the British Motor Corporation with none of the four works cars finishing. Paddy Hopkirk and Logan Morris both ran out of road and Timo Mäkinen smashed a wheel on a road-side distance marker.

Bad luck continued to dog the team during the Leige rally. Rauno Aaltonen crashed while leading the ultimate winner, Bohringer, by two minutes.

Timo Makinen seemed to be under the impression his pace notes for the Titograd section of the rally were exaggerating when they said, 'Unless you are absolutely mad, this section is quite impossible.' He hit a lorry while drifting his car sideways through a bend at 50 mph. Paddy Hopkirk stayed on the road, without hitting anything and finished in sixth place overall.

The Austin Healeys fared better in the RAC where Mäkinen and the Morleys finished first and second in their class respectively.

In March 1964 the definitive version of the Austin-Healey made its debut. The new MkIII BJ8 looked identical to the BJ7. Underneath the skin there was a variety of significant changes. The power output was further increased using a higher lift camshaft and twin 2 in. SU carburettors. A new exhaust system was fitted to meet expected West German noise regulations. The interior was completely redesigned with a polished veneer fascia and a lockable glove compartment. The rear seats were altered so that they could be folded flat to provide extra luggage space.

Production of the MkIII in this form was curtailed after just 390 examples had been made. While the new exhaust system reduced noise levels and increased power, it frequently did not stay on the car long enough for the owner to appreciate these benefits.

After ignoring complaints about the lack of ground clearance for over a decade, Austin were finally forced to do something about it.

The MkIII phase two had a 1 in. radiused section cut from the chassis where the rear axle was mounted. This allowed softer, six-leaf springs to be fitted. The axle itself was positively located with two radius arms to prevent wind up on acceleration. Uprated dampers completed the package. In one fell swoop the ride, handling and ground clearance were dramatically improved.

Why it took so long to resolve the Austin-Healey's niggling problems is easily explained. Austin never saw them as problems. The difficulty from the company's point of view was to supply enough cars to meet demand. Additional tooling costs and manufacturing delays were to be avoided as much as possible.

These modifications were introduced in March 1964 along with revised front and rear side lights. Later that year, following a number of stress fractures, the hub splines were reinforced to cope with the extra torque and the grip generated by new radial tyres. Separate indicators were fitted from 1965 onwards.

Despite these new features the tide was turning against the Austin-Healey. The car, while much modified, was still nearly 15 years old. The change in attitude was most noticeable in the Competition Department at the British Motor Corporation. The Mini was the rising star.

The Healey family decided to redress the balance by entering a car at Sebring in 1964. It finished the race in spectacular fashion – by somersaulting onto its roof after the driver, Grant Clark, lost control.

The new 3000 MkIII made its competition debut in the Tulip rally with the Morleys at the wheel. Once again they put in the best overall performance but lost out because of the event's class improvement system. Ironically, the winner was Mäkinen in a Mini Cooper S.

The Austrian Alpine and the French Alpine both showed the Austin-Healey was still as competitive as ever. Paddy Hopkirk won the Austrian outright while the Morleys collected a class win and a Coupe d'Argent (for their third, albeit non-consecutive, penalty-free run) in the French.

Left
Cosmetically the business end of the 100 Six differed little from that of the 3000. The Healey's styling was always acknowledged as one of its major assets. But it also made the car impossible to modify to meet US safety regulations

Right
The 3000 MkI was fitted with 11 in. discs

In its long career the Austin-Healey has notched up an impressive number of race and rally wins against far more exotic machines

Three Austin-Healeys were entered for the 1964 Leige which was to be the last. Rauno Aaltonen finished first but the other two entries were less fortunate. Paddy Hopkirk retired on the punishing Yugoslavia leg with just second gear working and Timo Mäkinen ran out of spare tyres when he was hit by a series of seven punctures. Mäkinen fared better in the RAC finishing second.

The works cars made their final appearance in 1965. The Morleys collected class wins in the Tulip, Geneva and Alpine rallies. Mäkinen repeated his previous success in the RAC. He led for much of the event but this time it was his turn to be pushed into second place by a Mini.

No works 3000s were entered in international events during 1966 and 1967 saw only one car available for competition use, the ex-Morley Alpine car. It was turned into the most potent ever road-going Austin-Healey for Rauno Aaltonen to drive in the RAC rally.

It featured an all aluminium engine, bored out to 2968cc, fitted with triple 45 DCOE Weber carburettors. Excess weight was cut to a minimum and the car tipped the scales at 24 cwt fully laden with nearly 200 bhp available at the wheels.

But an outbreak of foot and mouth disease put paid to Aaltonen's high hopes for his new car. The rally was cancelled at the eleventh hour amid fears that it could help spread the epidemic to livestock all over the country.

The Austin-Healey was denied its swan-song and production was phased out in March 1968.

TON 792 was the first right-hand-drive Austin-Healey produced

The triple carburettor layout used on competition Healeys was adopted by the 3000 MkII

The 3000 MkII featured a number of cosmetic styling changes designed to update it for the American market

Left
As the years passed the 3000 gradually gained more in the way of creature comforts

Above
Luggage space was always at a premium for Austin-Healey owners and boot racks were frequently fitted

NORTH AMERICAN CHALLENGE SERIES

June 22nd – 24th **MID OHIO** COLUMBUS, OHIO HEALEY MANIA WEEKEND	**July 3rd – 8th** **BLACK HAWK FARM RACEWAY** ROCKFORD, ILLINOIS CONCLAVE 1990	**July 20th – 22nd** **ROAD AMERICA** WISCONSIN
August 17th – 19th **LEGUNA SECA** CALIFORNIA	**September 1st – 2nd** **LIME ROCK** CONNECTICUT	**September 7th – 9th** **WATKINS GLEN** NEW YORK STATE

The 1990 Team Healey North American Challenge Series pitted some of the most famous cars and drivers in the Healey world against each other

Three of the nine Team Healey drivers who led the challenge against the American home team. Left to right Steve Bicknell, John Chatham and David Long

Above

DD 300 is one of the most historically important Austin-Healeys. It was first campaigned at Sebring in 1960 and has been winning races ever since. At Road America, however, John, 'went off playing with a GTO Ferrari and spun off.'
Note the GTO Ferrari in the background, 'red rag to a bull that was'

Right

The starting grid at the Blackhawk Farm stage of the North American Challenge. Left to right in the front ranks: Dan Pendergraft (US) in his 1957 100 Six, Roly Nix (GB) also in a 1957 100 Six, John Chatham (GB) in DD 300, Steve Bicknell (GB) in another 1957 100 Six and Phil Coombs (US) in his 1965 3000.

The five race series was all square before the final race at Watkins Glen. The heavens opened and John Chatham, King of the Wet, was nowhere to be found. The Americans were told he was drinking champagne, celebrating his victory. His prediction was accurate

Below
John Chatham is one of the best known Healey drivers. Pictured is one of his first cars, now fitted with a rather ropy V8

Left and above
Standard features on the rally cars were side exhausts for extra ground clearance and bugled boots to allow two spare wheels to be carried

Previous page
John Chatham's fun car GRX, pictured outside Cortina on the Pirelli Classic Marathon, is a long way removed from a standard Healey and is capable of nearly 150 mph. John is certain he was never picked as a work's driver because, 'I made made my cars go faster than theirs!'

Below
Pat Moss took URX 727 for a long test drive before she decided to buy it. She was behind the wheel for the 1960 Tulip, Alpine, Liege and German rallies

Peter Kuprianoff's 1960 3000, seen at the 1990 Austin-Healey Isle of White weekend where he beat John Chatham in a series of time trials. 'You have to be smooth,' commented Kuprianoff. 'We were watching you at the disco last night,' replied Chatham, 'and you were very smooth!' The 'tank commander' was the only German member of the British team during the Challenge Series

An Austin-Healey 3000 MkIII Phase Two

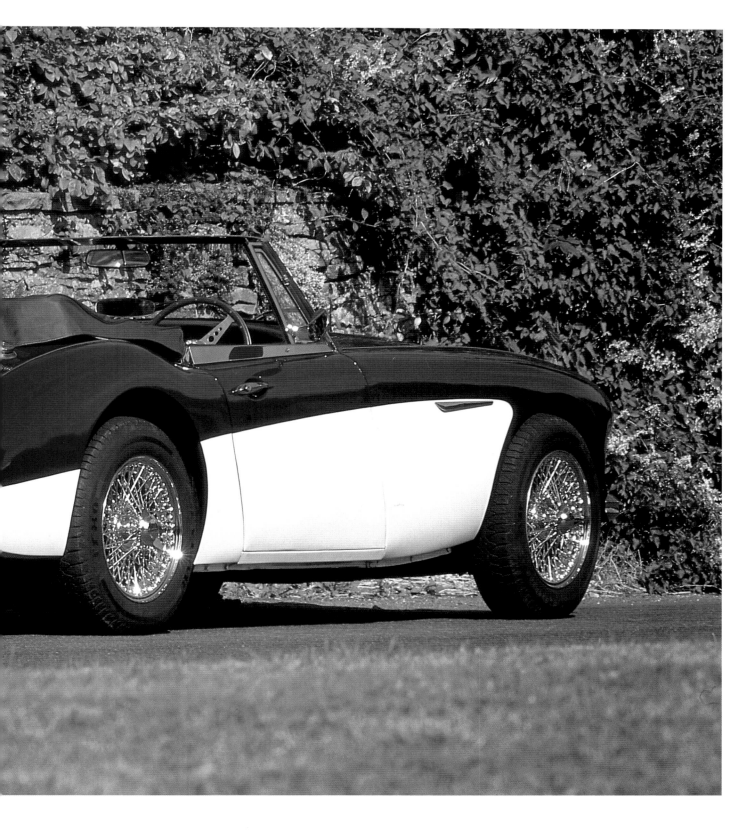

Moving with the times, the Austin-Healey 3000 MkIII Phase Two featured separate amber indicators

The sumptuous interior of the MkIII

Improved aerodynamics meant that the loss of one carburettor did not affect the overall performance

This view clearly shows the Austin-Healey's lack of ground clearance

The cause of so many of the Austin-Healey's problems: the chassis members ran under the rear axle, limiting the maximum ground clearance available

The 1964 Sebring car awaiting an engine rebuild after running its main bearings during the North American Challenge Series

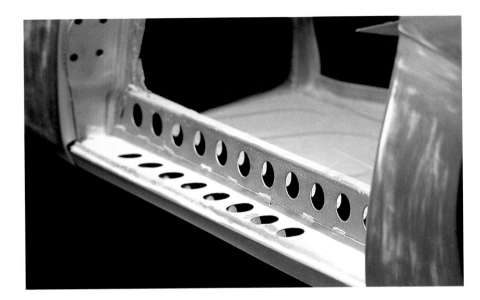

The car was designed to be as light as possible. This meant removing the window winder mechanism and drilling the sills to reduce weight

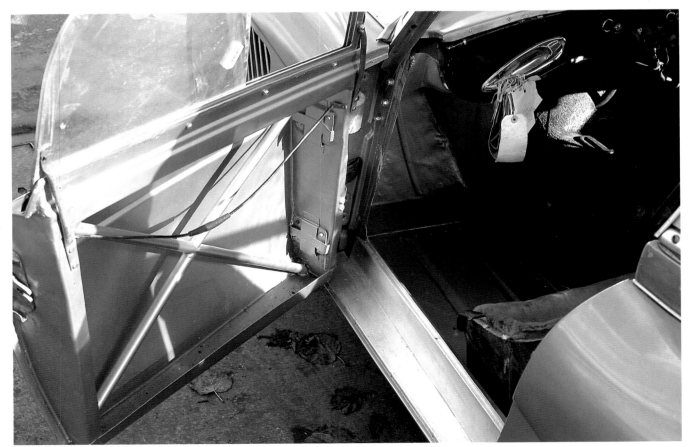

In simpler days, when the British Motor Corporation could see where it was going, Timo Mäkinen finished second overall in the 1965 RAC rally driving EJB 806C

The Big Healey and, waiting in the wings, its nemesis in rallying terms – the Mini

The end of the Affair

As early as 1960 discussions had been underway to find a suitable replacement for the 3000. By 1962 the British Motor Corporation was keen to rationalise production. The first proposal was to use a common body for both the 3000 replacement and an MG. It would have been very useful for the Corporation to have a large sports car badge-engineered in the same way as the Austin-Healey Sprite and the MG Midget.

A number of engine and body options were considered for the project. It was finally decided to use the updated C-Series engine, then under development, in a modified MGB body.

The new engine featured seven main bearings instead of the previous four. It also had a heavily revised cylinder head that was intended to meet all foreseeable American emission control regulations.

The combination of the new head and more internal friction meant that the engine actually produced less power than the old C-Series. It was also 70 lbs heavier than its design weight. The net result when installed in the MGB bodyshell was a nose heavy 56/44 weight distribution. Extensive alterations were also needed to shoehorn the unit into the engine bay. These had the advantage of making the shell more rigid but also a good deal heavier.

The final result was not impressive.

In fact it was so bad that there was talk of reviving the four-cylinder A90 unit originally used in the 100 Four. The block was still in production and a feasibility study was carried out into producing a new crankshaft and a twin-cam cylinder head.

When the MGC made its debut at the 1967 London Motor Show there was no Austin-Healey derivative. Donald and Geoff Healey wisely decide not to have anything to do with the ill-fated car which was withdrawn in September 1969.

While the MGC débâcle was unfolding they were working on their own plans for a 3000 replacement centred on the Rolls-Royce engined Austin-Healey 4000. The Rolls-Royce FB60 unit featured the classic Bentley inlet-over-exhaust valve layout. It delivered 175 bhp at 4,800 rpm when fed by twin 2 in. SU carburettors and, due to its alloy construction, was nearly 100 lbs lighter than the 3000's iron C-Series engine.

Rolls-Royce had set up lines capable of producing between 5,000 and 6,000 units a year under an engine supply deal with the British Motor Corporation. At the time only the Vanden Plas 4-litre R used the FB60 unit and it seemed there was a great deal of excess capacity available.

A twin-cam head had also been developed for the engine, giving approximately 268 bhp with triple SU carburettors.

In 1966 the Healey team in Warwick started assembling a prototype vehicle around the Rolls-Royce engine. Essentially they took a 3000 bodyshell and sliced it in two. A 6 in. fillet was added to give the extra width required by the 4-litre

Previous page

What might have been, if the Healeys had been allowed to develop the full potential of the 3000. DAC 130C was converted into a fixed-head coupé at Warwick. Its engine had an alloy head, high lift camshaft and triple SU carburettors. Disc brakes were fitted all round and the car was, in many ways, an embryonic 3000 S

Right

NAC 430F was built at Longbridge to assess which body panels could be rationalised with the current convertible's. The project was dropped when it was decided that a coupé version of the Big Healey would clash with the proposed MGC GT

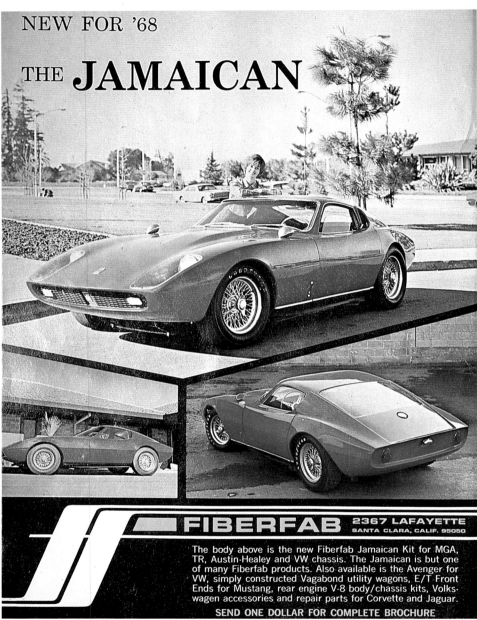

*One person's view of how the new Healey
should have looked. The Jamaican bears a
startling resemblance to the Datsun 240Z*

R rear axle. The removable fibre-glass transmission tunnel was replaced with a steel unit welded to the front and rear bulkheads. This enormously improved chassis rigidity and all but eliminated the scuttle shake which plagued all the Healeys. The chassis was then remade to accommodate the FB60 engine and a Borg-Warner Model 8 automatic gearbox.

Geoff Healey said, 'It was considered that there was a great market in the US for an automatic Healey and it would also use up BMC's stock of transmissions as well as of Rolls-Royce engines.'

Every effort was made to pre-empt American safety legislation. Rocker switches were used throughout and the 3000's veneer fascia was dropped. A collapsible steering column was also introduced which improved the driving position and created more space between the driver and the steering wheel. Standard springs and dampers were used which, when combined with the wider and stiffer body, gave significantly improved handling.

In February 1967 the completed prototype was delivered to Longbridge, the British Motor Corporation's headquarters, for evaluation.

The car's top speed, at 125 mph, was similar to the current 3000's. But the development potential of the Rolls-Royce unit, particularly when fitted with the twin-cam head was mouthwatering. In addition, all the worst faults of the 3000 model had been eliminated.

It was ordered into immediate production for launch in January 1968. Six pre-production cars were ordered to test transmission options – two with automatic

Above and right
A rather battered example of the Jamaican

Left
Probably the most photographed part of the Austin-Healey 4000. Originally the car just had a Healey badge. The Rolls-Royce emblem is taken from a keyring

Right
The first Healey 4000 prototype featured a bonnet bulge rather than the traditional air scoop. In reality it made little or no difference to under-bonnet temperatures

gearboxes, two with four-speed Jaguar E-Type units and two with Jaguar overdrive gearboxes.

In April 1967, with two of these cars nearing completion the whole project was cancelled. Why such a promising development was discarded is difficult to understand. A number of explanations have been offered.

Geoff Healey said, 'Unbeknown to us and to BMC, Rolls-Royce had suspected that BMC wouldn't be taking its full allocation of engines and had got rid of a lot of tooling, so it wasn't really in a position to start immediate production of the engine – certain critical castings weren't available.

'Also BMC was running out of money. The Corporation was in a very bad way. When it found its commitment to the engine disappear, and discovered there would be additional expenditure needed for tooling . . . .'

The 4000 was also a very different car from its predecessors. It had manners. The prestige of the refined Rolls-Royce engine, potentially scorching performance and good handling would have put the 4000 in direct competition with the E-Type Jaguar. And with a distinct price advantage.

There are suspicions that Sir William Lyons had more than a little to do with the demise of the project.

Other names crop up in the conspiracy theory. Geoff Healey points the finger at Lord Stokes, mastermind behind the Leyland and British Motor Corporation merger in 1967. 'He didn't like names on cars. He wanted it all to be British Leyland.'

Whatever the truth is, the 4000 was the last chance to produce a replacement for the Austin-Healey. The old C-Series engine was being deleted, the new C-Series engine was a disaster and impending American safety and emission regulations were just too much for the aging design to survive.

The cancellation of the 4000 effectively ended the 16 year partnership between the Healeys and Austin in all its guises.

The padded dashboard gives the Healey 4000 a very modern appearance

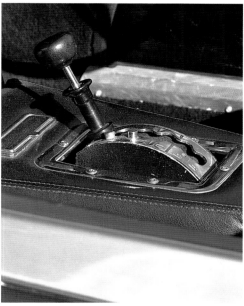

Above

*The 4000's poise and automatic gearbox
would have put it in a very different
market to the relatively cheap and
cheerful 3000*

Left

The 4-litre Roll-Royce engine

Healeys Today: Restoration

The decision to axe the Big Healey was considered by many a mistake. But then the 1960s and '70s are not often thought of as the halcyon days of Britain's car industry. During those years many of the names which Lord Stokes objected to disappeared. Today Triumph, Austin, Morris and Healey have all gone. Yet, the demand for their cars is still growing.

The Austin-Healey has achieved classic status and enthusiasts are quite prepared to pay five and six figure sums for good or rare examples, because they don't build cars like they used to. Many other motorists are enchanted by the Big Healey's looks but prefer something more modern, because they don't build cars like they used to.

John Chatham, a long established Healey specialist and racer said, 'I've never owned a MkIII for very long because after one long journey I never want to drive one again.'

The result of this demand for modernised Healeys has been the emergence of a number of firms specializing in fibre glass replicas using modern running gear. Many enthusiasts raise their hands in horror at the mention of kit-cars but the original Healey was essentially a kit-car – a custom-made chassis and body using the running gear from an existing production car.

Without Austin's backing Donald and Geoff Healey would have been just a small manufacturer not unlike Peter and Graham Holmes. They produce the Harrier, a 140 mph sports car with a Healey body.

Peter said, 'We finished our first prototype based on an MGB in 1985 and we initially imagined our market would be the kit car industry.

'We showed that at Silverstone and we found a tremendous amount of interest. We had 500 inquiries but it was quite apparent that nobody wanted a kit. So what we decided to produce was a completely new luxury car.

'We threw away the live rear axle and put in semi-trailing arms with coiled springs and telescopic dampers. We designed our own front suspension and then started work on the body. The windscreen and the doors had to be changed as well as both the shrouds.

'Originally we fitted a 3.5-litre Rover V8 engine. Then Rover just went up to the 3.9-litre engine. When you're in this business, using other people's components, you have development forced on you.

'We'd just sent drawings away to a wiring harness manufacturer and I didn't realise they'd changed the fuel injection system so that all had to be done again.

'Then the cooling system had to be changed because the fuel injection system had been changed. The repercussions are endless.

'I can see now why errors cropped up with the original Healeys. They didn't make those errors on purpose. You realise they usually had them forced on them and that what they designed was a compromise to start with.'

The Harrier is in many ways what the Austin-Healey 4000 might have been. Its 190 bhp engine gives it a top speed of 140 mph and it is equipped with every modern convenience including heated mirrors and electric windows.

Geoff Healey has given the project his blessing but Peter and Graham Holmes have been unable to adopt the Healey trade mark because of its disputed ownership.

The Scottish Haldane is possibly closer to the original concept of the Austin-Healey than the Harrier. Initially based on Vauxhall Chevette running gear, it has been redesigned to accept more readily available Ford components.

The car features a fully triangulated backbone chassis with wishbone suspension. Engine options include the Ford 2-litre Pinto and Toyota's twin-cam 1.6-litre unit.

Ironically 'Healeys' are now even being imported from America. The Cambridge-based firm Classic Car distribute the Saxon, the Sebring 5000 and the MX manufactured by Classic Roadsters Ltd of North Dakota. The Saxon is probably the most authentic of the three cars, featuring a straight six.

The appearance of the Sebring and the MX show the hand of a mod-sport designer in their styling and in the use of a 302 cu in V8 powerplant.

This proliferation of cars shows that the Healey shape is still as attractive today as it was over forty years ago. And the appearance of the Mazda MX5 in 1990 gave the motor industry a timely reminder that there is still a market for traditional sports cars even though Triumph, Austin, Morris and Healey have all gone.

The resurgence of interest in Austin-Healeys has led to more and more cars being restored. But while the vast majority of the parts needed are once again available, the job is not as straightforward as it might first appear.

Vehicles manufactured in the 1950s and 1960s are not renowned for their rustproofing and the main enemy when restoring cars of this vintage is corrosion.

The Big Healeys are by no means unusual in suffering from the dreaded 'tin worm'. Anyone who has worked on Jaguar MkIIs or Rover P5s will know that they rust just about everywhere. Unfortunately this is true of the majority of Big Healeys as well. The lower 12 in. are particularly prone to rust, especially if the car has lived in a damp and salty climate - like Britain.

If you are thinking of buying a Big Healey the most common places where they rust are the lower wing to chassis joints, the rear wings' lower cavity, the lower door, the inner and outer sills, the lower flange of the boot lid, the shut plates, the boot floor, the petrol tank and the tops of the wing. Electrolytic corrosion also occurs where the shroud meets the steel wings.

The outer front wings rot under the headlights and where they meet the bulkhead. The gap caused when the edges of the inner wings rust away allows road dirt to build up in this area, making the problem worse. This can often cause the lower portion of the wing to separate from its mounting. The rot rarely stops there though. It usually progresses to the sills, devouring both the inner and the outer before moving on.

Peter Ellis re-imported his rally replica as a wreck from America before restoring it and converting it to right-hand drive

The interior is slightly more luxurious
than that of an original works rally car

The 140 mph Harrier

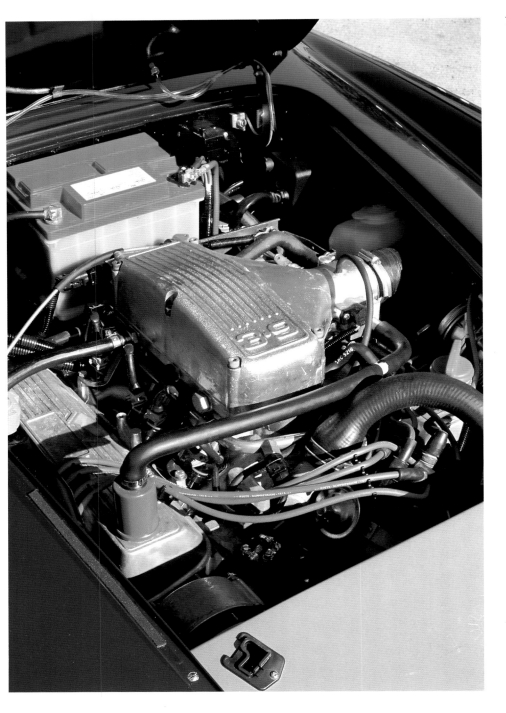

The Harrier's original 3.5-litre engine

The rear wings suffer similar problems. The rear wheels throw road dirt into the cavity between the wing and the shroud. This liberal coating of mud, salt and water causes the lower portion of the wing to rot away often taking the door shut face with it. There have been cases where the only thing holding the door shut area together has been the aluminium trim. The floor pan is also prone to corrosion, particularly across the front of the car and underneath the petrol tank.

The chassis and outriggers are not safe either. On the MkIII, the radius arms are mounted in boxes next to the wheel arches and these frequently rust away.

The front suspension pillars and engine mountings should also be checked. Loose shock absorbers have a nasty habit of parting company with the rest of the car and by the early 1970s many Austin-Healeys were showing signs of severe shock absorber mounting problems. Similarly the welds on the engine mountings can give up under the strain.

These are the areas of concern peculiar to the Austin-Healey. In general, beware of any car daubed in fresh underseal. It can hide a multitude of sins. The chassis should always be checked for true because, as Roger Bakewell said, 'You can throw a Healey down a straight at 100 mph. But try and get it round a bend and that's a bit different.' Quite a lot of Austin-Healeys have been bent at some stage in their careers. Often the chassis rails forward of the engine

The low profile 195/65/15 VR radials used make stowing the spare wheel a problem. The fuel tank is divided into two kidney shapes to accommodate it

Above
The Ford based Haldane

Left
The Harrier's interior has all the creature comforts that the modern motorist has come to expect, including heated mirrors and electric windows

mountings are distorted. The shape of the shroud around the radiator grill and bonnet should also be examined for signs of accident damage.

The typical 'Healey basket case' will basically need a new body and, as everyone knows, the bodywork is the expensive bit.

Very few amateur mechanics will have the either the expertise or the tools needed to build a completely new body. Unless you own a steel fabrication factory like Peter Ellis, this is a job best left to a professional restorer.

If you do feel confident enough to tackle the job, the first step is to strip the car completely. Removing the engine and gearbox as a unit can cause problems as a great deal of height is needed to give adequate clearance. Once the car has been stripped, and everything put away safely, the front and rear wings should be removed. Virtually all the body panels are now being re-manufactured and many restoration firms simply discard the old wings and replace them with new

The Saxon from Classic Roadsters, Fargo.
The interior trim is far more luxurious
than the original 3000, with a hardwood
dash and contour bucket seats

aluminium items. This cures the electrolytic corrosion problem. Where necessary the floor pan, inner and outer sills and outriggers are then cut away. The bare chassis is now ready for the attentions of a welder.

It is one of the laws of car maintenance that taking things apart is always much easier than putting them back together again. This is especially true of the Austin-Healey. John Chatham once said, 'It's a jigsaw and none of the pieces fit.'

The outriggers should be welded in first, squared up with the inner sill. The door should then be bolted to the door pillar. Usually these are fairly sound. With the door in position, the outer sill should be fitted, followed by the shut panel. Putting everything back in this order means that it all goes in square. The door assembly now acts as a guide for what follows.

Re-manufactured wings do not usually fit but then this was also true of the originals! Geoff Price, Healey's old service manager said, 'I can remember fitters trying four or five wings before they could get one to fit when the cars were being built.' Most of the re-manufactured wings are too long, some by a good half inch.

Another thing you have to watch out for are the swage lines. Often the curves do not line up, especially on the back wing. This can mean cutting the wing, re-shaping it and welding it back up again.

The chief problem with restoring these cars is the fact that essentially they were hand-built and no two are the same. It is a good idea to take measurements from the original panels before they are cut away. The new should always be checked against the old.

Mechanically there are far fewer problems with Austin-Healeys. Carroll Shelby was certain that the engine 'must have been directly descended from a 1918 London bus' and 'agricultural' is the fond endearment used by most Healey enthusiasts.

Needless to say the engine in an Austin-Healey is not very highly stressed and

The Sebring, named after the Healey's favourite venue. ¼ mile in 12.8 seconds for the MX model which compares pretty well with 15.1 for the Porsche 944 Turbo!

The MX chassis and running gear

they are fairly reliable. But, like all cars, they do not take kindly to neglect.

Low oil pressure and high oil consumption are common in older engines. Cylinder bore wear will cause crankcase compression with a resultant oil mist collecting in the filter. Cam followers frequently lose their case hardening and, as George Darbyshire, an engine restorer with Healey specialist JME, put it, 'the rockers and rocker shafts are always worn to hell! You have to re-face the rockers and re-do the shafts too. You get a bit of distributor drive and oil pump drive wear as well, and you have to watch that a bit.'

Once the crankshaft has been re-ground, the block re-bored, the rockers re-faced and new main and big end bearings fitted that is about it really! 'But you've got to do all these bits and bobs on them.'

Overhauling the engine of an Austin-Healey is well within the capabilities of a reasonably competent mechanic although the sheer weight of the unit can cause some headaches.

The majority of parts are available although tracking down things like oversize pistons can hold work up. Many crankshafts are now reaching maximum re-grind and 100 Four cylinder heads are becoming quite scarce due to internal cracks.

Fortunately for Austin-healey owners there are other alternatives available. The crankshaft, block and con rods from the A105 Austin Westminster are interchangeable with those in BN4 models. The BN6 abandoned the integral inlet manifold used on this engine and had a special cylinder head. Ironically, police Westminsters of the time were also fitted with this Healey head.

The crankshaft and con rods from the A70 are identical to those used in the 100 Four and the cylinder head can be altered to the correct specification.

Moving on to the transmission, overdrives are fairly robust and trouble free. The main problems are external; misadjustment, a defective solenoid or loose electrical connections. There is no synchromesh on first gear and the laygear frequently suffers because of this. Weak rear springs are another common problem. If the wheel is disappearing into the arch then there is some cause for concern. Removing them can cause problems as the front hanger bolt often rusts solid to the sleeve it passes through. With the wing in place there just is not enough room to swing a hammer to knock it out. Short hard taps with a small hammer are needed if damage to the wing is to be avoided.

Restoring an Austin-Healey completely will take a skilled enthusiast as a very rough rule of thumb about three years and a professional approximately nine months. It is not something to be undertaken lightly.

Interest in Healeys is now such that virtually no car is beyond redemption on economic grounds

Above
The floor pan has been cut away from this badly rotted chassis

Left
The drier climate in America means export models have tended to fair better in terms or rust than their British counterparts

On a Healey there is no such thing as localised corrosion

The massive torque generated by the
Healey's engine can cause the engine
mountings to walk. Welding in extra
gussets prevents this

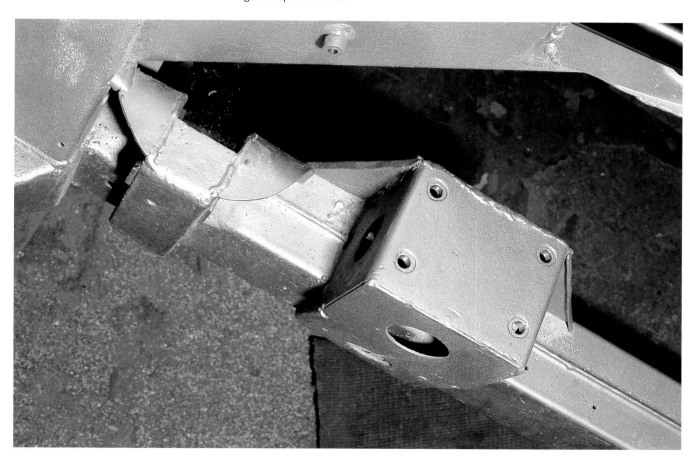

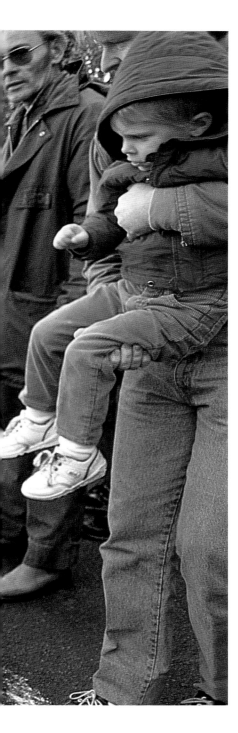

Left

Many Healeys came to grief in the 1970s. This one crashed a little more recently. This Healey's chassis was badly corroded and concertinaed on impact. The full extent of the damage was not apparent, however until the vehicle was inspected on a ramp

Below

New metal often has to be welded in to repair doors

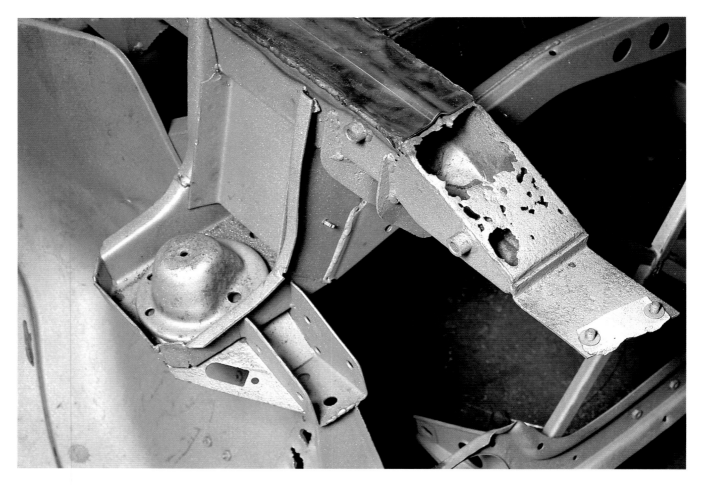

Above

A badly corroded chassis rail can be repaired by capping

Left

This radius arm mounting box has been bodged. The only answer with rust is to cut it out and weld in new metal

The Healey's steering is complex and a great deal of wear can build up in the joints causing excessive play at the steering wheel

Measure up all the panels before you start cutting; this gives you a guide to work to when putting on the new panels

Most of the components for the Healey are now remanufactured. Except for the horn boss which is the only thing in need of restoration on this example

Many of the parts from the A105 Austin Westminster engine are interchangeable with those of the A90

Few of the parts on the engine pictured are likely to be interchangeable with any standard Austin unit. This ex-works all alloy competition engine is only one of three ever made. It is currently in residence at the bottom of John Chatham's garden. Occasionally a 'new' Healey appears from his store of spares but this engine is intended for something special. Note the lightened flywheel

Above
A bare metal respray must of course be in a dust free environment

Overleaf
Completely restoring a car requires a lot of room and an enclosed garage